D0646928

Getting To Know...

Nature's Children

ANTS

Caroline Greenland

PUBLISHER	Joseph R. DeVarennes
PUBLICATION DIRECTOR	Kenneth H. Pearson
MANAGING EDITOR	Valerie Wyatt
SERIES ADVISOR	Merebeth Switzer
SERIES CONSULTANT	Michael Singleton
CONSULTANTS	Ross James
	Kay McKeever
	Dr. Audrey N. Tomera
ADVISORS	Roger Aubin
	Robert Furlonger
	Gaston Lavoie
EDITORIAL SUPERVISOR	Jocelyn Smyth
PRODUCTION MANAGER	Ernest Homewood
PRODUCTION ASSISTANTS	Penelope Moir
	Brock Piper

EDITORS

Katherine Farris	Anne Minguet-Patocka
Sandra Gulland	Sarah Reid
Cristel Kleitsch	Cathy Ripley
Elizabeth MacLeod	Eleanor Tourtel
Pamela Martin	Karin Velcheff

PHOTO EDITORS	Bill Ivy
	Don Markle
DESIGN	Annette Tatchell
CARTOGRAPHER	Jane Davie
PUBLICATION ADMINISTRATION	Kathy Kishimoto
	Monique Lemonnier

ARTISTS

Marianne Collins	Greg Ruhl
Pat Ivy	Mary Theberge

This series is approved and recommended by the Federation of Ontario Naturalists.

Canadian Cataloguing in Publication Data

Greenland, Caroline.
  Ants

(Getting to know—nature's children)
Includes index.
ISBN 0-7172-1914-3

1. Ants—Juvenile literature.
I. Title. II. Series.

QL568.F7G73 1985   j595.796   C85-098701-6

Have you ever wondered . . .

The next time you have a picnic on a hot summer day, see how long it takes you to spot an ant. Chances are one of these remarkable little insects will be crawling over your tablecloth in a matter of minutes. Ants have an uncanny ability to find you and your food in record time, don't they?

And that's not the only amazing thing about ants. They have an incredible determination to survive in the face of obstacles that would stop most people. Imagine coming out of your home each day to face pushing your way through a thick forest and scaling the Empire State Building or the CN Tower. That is what an ant does when it runs through a forest of grass and then up a plant stem.

Ants are also surprisingly strong. What other animal do you know that can carry up to 27 times its own weight and not even puff?

But perhaps the most amazing thing about the ant is the way it co-operates with its fellow ants for the good of the whole ant colony. It is this co-operation that makes the ant one of the most interesting creatures in the animal world.

Ants Everywhere

Have you got ants in your backyard or house? Most likely you do. No matter where you live in North America—in rainy coastal areas, in a desert, on a mountain, in a forest—there are ants there too.

Ants have lived on earth for millions of years. Long ago they were found only in the hot tropical areas of the world. But today there are ants everywhere, except in the extremely cold arctic and subarctic lands.

In all, there are over 35,000 kinds of ants in the world. Some are as large as a new eraser —up to six centimetres (two and a half inches) long. Others are so small that they are difficult to see.

Ants come in a range of colors, too. They can be brown, yellow, red or black—but black ants are the most common.

Red ant colony.

Ants Are Insects

All ants are part of a much bigger animal group, namely insects. Within this large group, their closest relatives are wasps and bees. In fact, some wasps look very much like ants!

Like all adult insects, ants have six legs and three separate parts to their bodies. The first part is the head, which has two feelers called antennae. The middle section is the thorax, and the last part is the abdomen. The next time you see a creepy crawly, give it the insect test. Count the legs and the body parts. Is it an insect? You may have found a spider or a centipede instead!

Also like other insects, an ant does not have lungs. It takes in air through small holes called spiracles along the sides of its thorax and abdomen. The air passes into small breathing tubes that branch through all parts of its body.

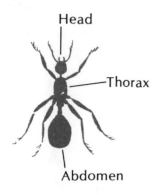

Head
Thorax
Abdomen

A Life Full of Changes

An ant will pass the insect test with flying colors. But ants do not always look like the six-legged creatures we see in our gardens. During their lives they go through several changes. This process of change is called metamorphosis. At times during their metamorphosis ants look very un-antlike indeed.

They start life as tiny white eggs. Out of these hatch wormlike grubs called larvae. The larva spins itself a cocoon where it undergoes even more changes. At this cocoon stage it is called a pupa. Finally it is ready to emerge from its cocoon as an adult ant, looking the way we expect ants to look. Inside the cocoon it has developed legs, antennae and all the necessary body parts.

As soon as it breaks out of the cocoon it is ready to takes its place in the ant colony.

Ant Armor

An ant is entirely covered by a tough overcoat that is just like armor. The knights of old had to put on armor for protection, but an ant's armor, or exoskeleton, is built right in.

The exoskeleton is made up of a material called chitin, which is very much like the stuff our fingernails are made of. And just as the bones in your skeleton give you shape, an ant's exoskeleton gives it shape too.

Don't be fooled: despite their frail appearance ants are quite hardy.

Ant Antennae

Next time you see an ant, watch how it moves its antennae. You may see it wave them in the wind or tap the ground all around it. What is it doing? It may be smelling for food, testing for wetness, feeling for vibrations or even taking the temperature! As you have probably guessed by now, an ant's antennae give it all its information about the world.

If you could look at an antenna under a microscope, you would see rows of tiny bumps up and down its length. These bumps pick up scents, and so the ant can actually smell with its antennae. By touching with its feelers, an ant can thoroughly inspect its food or feel its way through the maze of tunnels that makes up its home. The ant does not have good vision. After all, good sight is not so necessary if you have a pair of antennae, is it?

You can tell that the antennae are very important to the ant by the great care it gives them. An ant is constantly cleaning them with its mouth and legs. In fact, there are special combs on the ant's legs for this very purpose.

Opposite page:

All ants have elbowed antennae.

12

Warning System

An ant's antennae also act as danger detectors.
They pick up vibrations from the ground. If
an ant senses strange vibrations, it scoots off,
out of harm's way. This makes sneaking up on
an ant difficult.

For extra safety, the ant has a back-up
warning system. It has hair-like spikes all over
its exoskeleton. These "hairs" come out
through the tough outer shell and are attached
to nerves under its surface. When anything
touches them, even a breeze, the ant takes
note. If it thinks an enemy is near, away it
runs to safety.

*The ant's powerful jaws open and
close sideways.*

Neat Feet

Have you ever wondered how an ant can walk on a ceiling and not fall on its head? It is simple. Each of the ant's six legs has five flexible segments and ends with a pair of tiny claws. When an ant walks up or down something like a wall, or across a surface upside down, these tiny claws hook themselves into cracks and bumps. There are very few surfaces that are too smooth for an ant to walk on. Even something like glass, that appears perfectly smooth to us, has ripples and crevices large enough for an ant's claws to grab onto.

In addition to the claws at the end of its legs, an ant also has claws higher up on its legs, above the first segment. These point towards the tip of the leg, and provide extra support when needed.

Machine Mouth

You mainly use your mouth for talking and eating. Believe it or not, some ants use their mouths as weapons and some use them as tools for carving out tunnels through earth or into wood. And of course, an ant uses its mouth for eating too.

No matter what their use, all ants' mouths are similar. They are simply holes in the front of their heads! Instead of having lips and a jaw like yours, an ant has hard pieces of exoskeleton at the edges of its mouth. These pieces swing together, like pairs of ice tongs to close the hole.

While an ant does have a tongue, it does not have teeth. Who needs teeth when you have hardened "lips" to cut and bite and hold with?

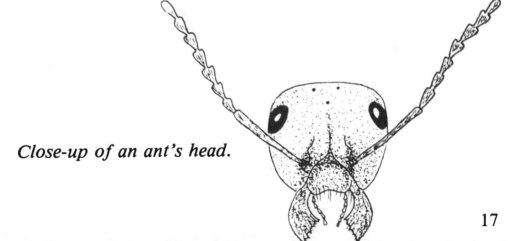

Close-up of an ant's head.

Storage Stomachs

Ants have to share their food. And what better way to carry it back to the colony than in their stomachs? Ants have a two-part stomach. In one part, food for the colony is temporarily stored. This stomach is called the crop. In the other part is the ant's own personal supply of food.

When an ant finds food, it chews it up and dissolves it in a liquid. Most of this liquid food goes into the crop, and a very small bit goes into the other part of the ant's stomach for its own use.

Back at the colony, the ant with the full crop helps feed the others. Now that's sharing!

Some ants collect the sweet-tasting juice which oozes from the tiny aphid.

Colony Life

One ant by itself would not live long. Perhaps that is why you rarely see a single ant. There is always another one close by. And another. And another. But it is not their numbers that make ants different from other insects—it is their organization. Ants live in colonies that vary in size from a dozen to thousands upon thousands of ants. Within these colonies, ants co-operate with each other, much the same as people do in cities or towns.

In most colonies there are three different types, or castes, of ants. Each caste looks different from the others and has a different contribution to make to the colony.

Size comparison

Worker

Male

Queen

The first caste is made up of queen ants. There is usually only one queen per colony. The queen is larger than the other ants and, for the first part of her life, has wings. Her job is twofold. First she is responsible for founding a new colony, and secondly, she must lay the eggs to produce new ants to keep the colony going.

The second caste is made up of winged male ants. They only have one job to perform in their very short lives—they must mate with a queen and fertilize her eggs. After mating they die.

The third caste is made up of the female worker ants. These are the ants you most commonly see. The survival of the colony ultimately rests on their shoulders, although it is the queen that begins the whole process.

slave raiders carrying off young

tending pupae

guest fly larvae

tending larvae

mutual feeding

tending a queen

a beetle guest

nest of thief ants

gathering honeydew from aphids

bringing in food

digging new tunnels

resting and grooming

This illustration shows some of the activities that go on inside the underground nest of a common ant. The life of the ant colony centers on the queen, or queens. Each queen is constantly fed and groomed by the workers, and the eggs that she lays are carried off to chambers where they hatch into tiny larvae. The larvae and the pupae into which they develop are also continually cleaned and fed. Within the nest there may be "guest" insects, such as fly larvae and beetles.

The workers spend much of their time in housekeeping activities. They also dig and maintain tunnels, clean, groom and feed each other, and collect food. Foraging ants are constantly bringing food into the nest. The workers are also always ready to defend the colony against intruders, including slave-making ants who often raid the nest.

Mating Flight

Imagine that you are sitting outside on a warm summer evening. Suddenly the air around you is filled with flying ants. You are witnessing the mating flight that will start a new ant colony.

In one gigantic whirring insect cloud, the young queens and the male ants fly high above the ground to mate. After an hour or so, they fly back down to earth. The males' brief but vital task is accomplished. Soon they will die. But the queen's lifetime work is just beginning.

The winged male ants are only born at certain times of the year.

All Hail the Queen

The queen must find a suitable place for her colony-to-be. As soon as she does, her wings fall off. She no longer needs them.

Next the queen busies herself by tunneling underground to make a nest. All alone, she seals herself into her tunnel and starts to lay eggs.

Now comes a long, lonely time of waiting, sometimes as long as nine months. During this period the queen tends and licks her eggs carefully. Once they have hatched, she feeds the larvae with her very own saliva, which has food value. You may wonder how she feeds herself. Believe it or not, she absorbs her now useless wing muscles for food and occasionally eats a few of the smaller eggs.

The queen ant is the mother of the colony. She may live up to 15 years.

Hatch Time

Once the ants have hatched and undergone their metamorphosis from grublike larvae to adult ants, they are ready to help their queen set up a colony. Now the queen can settle back and receive the royal treatment she richly deserves. She will be taken care of completely so that she is free to carry out her main task for the colony—laying eggs.

The workers' most important task is to find food. Some go out immediately. Soon they return and pass the food they have gathered in their crops to the queen and then to the larvae. Other workers clean the eggs and care for the new larvae and pupae. Meanwhile still others busily dig out new tunnels to enlarge the colony's home.

This nursery worker is kept very busy cleaning and feeding the larvae.

Home Sweet Home

You may well have seen many ant homes and never given them a second thought. Remember those small mounds of earth, bare of grass with lots of holes poked into the top surface? If you saw ants scurrying in and out of these holes, however, you probably guessed that you were looking at an ant home.

Many North American ants live in underground nests, which look like miniature mountains above ground. But below ground is a complicated system of tunnels and rooms—a whole city in fact!

Depending upon the type of ant, there may be storerooms for seeds, fungus or nectar. There will be nursery chambers where workers care for the eggs, larvae and pupae. There might even be a series of empty rooms where the young can be moved in case the nest is damaged or attacked. And of course, there is the royal suite, where the queen lives.

The ground is not the only place for an ant home. Can you guess where a carpenter ant lives? That's right, in wood. They can be

found in dead logs, stumps, or if you are really unlucky, even in your house. If you find little piles of sawdust under a hole in your woodwork, chances are that you have carpenter ants living with you.

Other ants build simple homes high up in trees or under rocks, while still others burrow under tree roots and dig out elaborate underground "apartment buildings."

Like caterpillars, some ant larvae spin cocoons around themselves. Inside they change into adults.

Chemical Kisses

How on earth do all of the thousands of ants know what to do and when to do it? In their own special way, they are actually taking orders from their queen. She is constantly letting out special chemical substances that are passed on to her workers when they lick her clean. In turn, these ants pass on the substances by a sort of kiss.

When an ant touches another ant's mouth, it picks up these and other chemicals that give it information. It learns if the other ant is from its home colony, what it has been eating and what job the ant performs. In short, these "kisses" are the secret to the ant colony's organization. They bind the colony together and enable it to survive.

Even when an ant is still in the egg or pupal stage, it communicates by giving off chemical messages. At this time the message is likely to be "Get me out of here." When the nursery workers smell this signal, they rush to the aid of the egg or pupa and tear open its case to let the larva or adult out.

Finding Food

Being able to find food is essential to every living creature, and ants are no exception. Here again, these little insects are good at helping each other for the benefit of the whole colony. For instance, if one leaf-cutting ant returns to the nest with a leaf from a lush patch of plants, she immediately tells the other workers. She runs about striking them with her antennae. The message here is "Hurry up." She knows the scent trail she has laid down all the way from the plants to the nest only lasts minutes. If the other ants hurry, they will be able to backtrack along her trail before it disappears. And then they too will be able to take advantage of the new food source.

To an ant, there is no such word as can't!

Farming Ants

For all they enjoy the treats you might take along on a picnic, ants are far from dependent upon you and your picnic basket for food.

Some ants are farmers. The leaf-cutting ants of Louisiana and Texas take leaves into their underground nests and grow a special fungus, or kind of mushroom, on them. The fungus thrives in the darkness of the nest and the ants eat it whenever they are hungry. This means the ants only have to leave the safety of their nests when they need more leaves.

Still other ants are dairy farmers. They tend aphids the way dairy farmers tend cows. Aphids are tiny insects that feed on plant juices. They suck up more juice than they need, so the ants take advantage of the surplus. Softly they stroke the backs of the aphids with their antennae. Out come tiny drops of honeydew that the ants store in their crops. It is a convenient arrangement: the ant gets the sweet food for its colony, and the aphid is protected from other insects by having the ants around.

Opposite page:

Although carpenter ants chew tunnels through wood, they do not eat any of it.

Different Tastes

Carpenter ants have different tastes. Although these large dark ants spend their lives busily chewing long tunnels through wood, they do not eat the wood itself. Instead, like fire ants, they have a varied diet. They capture and consume insects, eat seeds or suck the juices from rotting fruit, vegetables or flowers.

Other ants, known as harvester ants, live up to their name by gathering or harvesting seeds. They carefully fill special storerooms in their mounds with great quantities of seeds. Then they actually mill the seeds by crushing them with their large, strong jaws. All this chewing results in a sort of bread, which feeds all the ants in the colony.

Sometimes the seeds start to sprout before they can be chewed. These thrifty ants quickly carry them outside the mound and leave them to grow. In time the plants will provide the ants with a handy supply of seeds. No wonder they are called harvester ants!

Living Honeypots

Perhaps the strangest food habits of all can be found among the honey ants. These ants live in the dry plains and deserts of the western United States. Like many ants, their diet is made up of honeydew from other insects, nectar from flowers and other plant juices. But unlike many ants, they often have dry desert conditions to contend with, and food is not always available.

In preparation for the lean times, honey ants store food in a very special way. Believe it or not, some worker ants in the colony actually become containers for extra food! When times are good, these ants are fed until they can barely move. Then they hang from the ceiling of the nest until they are needed. In dry periods, they are tapped for food to keep the colony alive. In essence they are living honeypots!

Ant Against Ant

An ant's most worrisome enemy is often other ants. Fierce battles sometimes break out between neighboring colonies or different kinds of ants. Most of the large ant battles occur in southern ant colonies. For some reason, northern ants are not so aggressive.

What do they fight about? Are they defending their nests? Or are they protecting the surrounding territory that they need for gathering food? Whatever the reason, thousands of worker ants will fight for hours—tumbling, biting and pulling at each other. New ant reinforcements find the battlegrounds quickly by following scent trails. But strangely enough, very few ants get hurt or killed during these scuffles.

Apart from these battles, some ants are actually hunted, killed and eaten by other ants.

A fight to the finish.

Watch Out, Ants!

It goes without saying that many lizards, birds and insect-eating mammals take their toll of ant lives each year. Some ants even have to watch out for a particularly crafty enemy called the antlion.

Do not let the name fool you! The antlion is neither an ant nor a lion. It is an insect that looks very much like a small dragon. When this insect is in its larval stage, it burrows into the soil, making a steepsided pit as it goes. Finally it is completely covered except for its jaws, which poke up through the sand in the bottom of the pit. Here it waits for an ant or other insect to fall in and provide it with a tasty snack!

Another ant predator is the tiger beetle. It uses much the same tactics as the antlion. But instead of waiting for the ant to fall into a pit, the tiger beetle leaps out of its hiding hole like a jack-in-the-box. The ant is then hauled back into the burrow.

Opposite page:

Ants regularly use their tongue to lick themselves clean.

Ants on Guard

Naturally all ants are fiercely protective of their colony, and they will die to defend their queen. The main defense of most ants is their bite. But many, like the fire ant, can give a painful sting too.

Other ants, such as wood ants, can shoot a bad smelling liquid at attackers, much the way a skunk does. This stinky spray discourages even a hungry animal from making a meal of a wood ant!

On guard!

Thank You, Ants

Some people find ants rather a bother. After all, some of them bite, don't they? And they can be annoying at picnics—right? And their appetite for plants can even harm some farmers' crops. But ants have many good points too.

For one thing they are fascinating and fun to watch. For another, they show how well things can work if everyone co-operates. But, more importantly, they also help improve the soil by tunneling through it. They break down dead plant material and add air to the soil. This is just like having free gardening service coast to coast. So the next time you see one of these amazing little ants—don't stand in its way, it has a job to do!

Special Words

Abdomen   The tail section of an insect's body.

Antennae   Feelers attached to the ant's head.

Caste   Grouping of ants according to the function they perform in the colony.

Chitin   Hard material that forms the ant's exoskeleton.

Cocoon   The covering for the ant pupa in which it develops into an adult ant.

Colony   A group of ants led by a queen.

Crop   Part of an ant's stomach where it stores food that is to be used by the other colony members.

Exoskeleton   The hard outer covering of an ant's body.

Larva   The second stage in an ant's life after it has hatched from the egg.

Metamorphosis   The process of change from egg to adult ant.

Nectar   The sweet liquid produced by plants.

Pupa   The stage of the ant's life when it is in its cocoon.

Thorax   The mid-section of an insect's body.

INDEX

Cover Photo: Bill Ivy

Photo Credits: Bill Ivy, pages 4, 10, 13, 14, 25, 26, 29, 31, 37, 40, 43, 44;
Kennon Cooke (Valan Photos), pages 7, 34; Val and Alan Wilkinson (Valan
Photos), page 18; John Fowler (Valan Photos), page 32. Illustration on pages
22-23 by Arabelle Wheatley, courtesy of *Encyclopedia Americana*.

Getting To Know...

Nature's Children

WEASELS

Bill Ivy

PUBLISHER	Joseph R. DeVarennes
PUBLICATION DIRECTOR	Kenneth H. Pearson
MANAGING EDITOR	Valerie Wyatt
SERIES ADVISOR	Merebeth Switzer
SERIES CONSULTANT	Michael Singleton
CONSULTANTS	Ross James
	Kay McKeever
	Dr. Audrey N. Tomera
ADVISORS	Roger Aubin
	Robert Furlonger
	Gaston Lavoie
EDITORIAL SUPERVISOR	Jocelyn Smyth
PRODUCTION MANAGER	Ernest Homewood
PRODUCTION ASSISTANTS	Penelope Moir
	Brock Piper
EDITORS	Katherine Farris, Anne Minguet-Patocka
	Sandra Gulland, Sarah Reid
	Cristel Kleitsch, Cathy Ripley
	Elizabeth MacLeod, Eleanor Tourtel
	Pamela Martin, Karin Velcheff
PHOTO EDITORS	Bill Ivy
	Don Markle
DESIGN	Annette Tatchell
CARTOGRAPHER	Jane Davie
PUBLICATION ADMINISTRATION	Kathy Kishimoto
	Monique Lemonnier
ARTISTS	Marianne Collins, Greg Ruhl
	Pat Ivy, Mary Theberge

This series is approved and recommended by the Federation of Ontario Naturalists.

Canadian Cataloguing in Publication Data

Ivy, Bill, 1953-
    Weasels

(Getting to know—nature's children)
Includes index.
ISBN 0-7172-1913-5

1. Weasel—Juvenile literature.
I. Title.   II. Series.

QL737.C25I95 1985   j599.74'447   C85-098742-3

Have you ever wondered . . .

Few animals have such a poor reputation as weasels. It seems that no one loves them. To call someone a "weasel" is quite an insult, since weasels are thought to be cruel and sneaky. But do weasels really deserve all this bad publicity?

If you took a close look at a weasel you might be in for a surprise. The first thing you would notice would be the weasel's bright black eyes and intelligent-looking face. It doesn't look sneaky at all—just alert and watchful. A closer look at how this small creature lives might reveal even more surprises.

Unlikely Relatives

The weasel is a member of a very large and interesting animal family. It bears a strong family resemblance to its closest cousins—the fisher, marten and mink— but some of its more distant relatives might come as a surprise. Among these are the skunk, badger, otter and wolverine.

One thing that most members of this family have in common is beautiful, silky coats.

The markings on the face of southern Long-tailed Weasels have earned them the name "bridled weasel."

Long-tailed Weasel dressed in its winter finery.

6

Three Weasels

Weasels live in most of North America, Europe and Asia. Some even live as far south as South America and northern Africa.

Although there are about ten different kinds of weasels in the world, only three make their home in Canada and the United States—the Long-tailed Weasel, the ermine and the Least Weasel.

Least Weasel

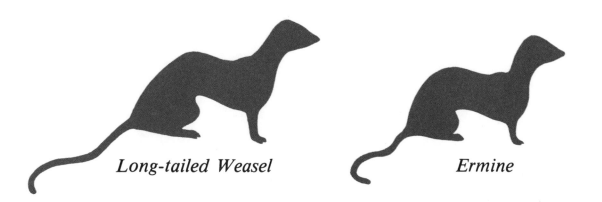

Long-tailed Weasel   *Ermine*

Even though it is North America's largest weasel, the Long-tailed Weasel weighs less than half a kilogram (one pound)!

Long-tailed Weasel

Can you guess how the Long-tailed Weasel got its name? Of course—because it has a very long tail, almost a third of its total length. From the tip of its nose to the end of this long tail, a male Long-tailed Weasel measures about 55 centimetres (21 inches). This makes it the largest of the three North American weasels. The female is considerably smaller than the male.

In the summer, the Long-tailed Weasel's fur is cinnamon-brown on the upper part with yellowish white undersides. In the southern part of its range it bears a black-and-white face mask that looks rather like a bridle and has earned it the name of "bridled weasel."

The Long-tailed Weasel is active at night and does its sleeping during the day. It is a good swimmer and always lives close to water.

Where Long-tailed Weasels live in North America.

The Long-tailed Weasel can climb a tree quietly enough to surprise a roosting bird.

The Ermine

Some people think that the ermine is white all year round. This is not so. In the summer, the ermine is a lovely chocolate brown color with white front feet and belly. Its black-tipped tail is not very long and accounts for only one-quarter of its total length of 21 to 33 centimetres (8-13 inches).

Unlike the other two weasels that live in North America, the ermine is sometimes active during the day. But like the others, it is very fearless and will not hesitate to climb a tree or take to the water while hunting. This bold little creature will sometimes even venture into a cabin to dine on leftover kitchen scraps.

Where ermine live in North America.

The ermine is also known as the Short-tailed Weasel.

Least Weasel

The Least Weasel is tiny, as its name suggests. Only 18 to 20 centimetres (7-8 inches) long and weighing about 43 grams (one and a half ounces), it is one of the smallest meat-eaters in the world. It is no larger than many of the mice it hunts and smaller than some of its prey. Like most weasels, though, it is bold and fearless. In fact its Latin name *rixosa* means quarrelsome.

The Least Weasel is quite rare and is very seldom seen. It has an attractive walnut-brown color set off by bright white underparts and feet.

Where Least Weasels live in North America.

Because of its small size, the Least Weasel is also called the pygmy weasel.

Weasel Homes

Weasels live in grasslands, woods, marshes and farmlands—wherever there is plenty of food.

Some live in hollow logs and stumps, while others take over other animals' underground burrows and "redecorate" them. Usually this means enlarging the den and adding extra entrances. When they are done the den may have three rooms—a bedroom, toilet and food storage room. To make its bedroom comfortable, the weasel may line it with grass and with fur plucked from its prey (which often includes the burrow's previous owner!).

If no natural site is available, weasels will sometimes move in with people. They will make their homes in the crawl spaces under buildings or in unused corners of barns.

Who goes there? (Least Weasel)

Where's the Weasel?

If you have ever seen a weasel in the wild consider yourself lucky—few people have. Why are weasels so difficult to spot? One reason is that they are usually active after sunset. Another is their small size and speediness. Even the largest of the weasels usually weighs less than 270 grams (half a pound), and this small bundle rarely walks—it bounds. So if you are walking in the country one evening and see a small furry blur out of the corner of your eye, try to take a closer look. It might be a weasel.

The weasel knows how to stay out of sight. Although you do not see it, chances are it is watching you.

Change of Clothes

Just like you, weasels have different winter and summer wardrobes. During the summer they have a rich brown coat with a lighter colored belly. But in the fall, the fur on their heads, backs and sides takes on a "salt and pepper" look. Gradually, as winter approaches, the brown hairs are shed, and white hairs grow in their place.

Weasels' winter coats blend in perfectly with the snow. This allows them to scamper about without being seen. Not only can they sneak up on their prey with ease but also they are less visible to their enemies.

When spring comes, dark hairs once again appear along the weasels' backs and sides. Before too long, they are fully outfitted in their summer browns.

In the southern parts of their range where snow rarely falls, weasels do not need a white winter coat. They wear their brown coats all year round.

Two Layered Coat

No matter what the time of year, weasels always have a double fur coat. Close to the weasel's body is a layer of thick inner fur. This keeps in body heat in the winter. To keep water off this layer of fur, the weasel has long guard hairs that are over the underfur.

As you might expect, the weasel's summer coat is much shorter and less dense than its winter coat. After all, who needs a big fur coat in mid-summer?

Glow-in-the-dark eyes.

Little Stinker

Would you believe that any animal could smell worse than a skunk? Some people claim that weasels do! Their foul-smelling odor is caused by a liquid known as musk. Unlike skunks, weasels cannot spray their enemies with musk. However, the terrible smell they give off when frightened or excited is enough to discourage many animals from attacking.

Weasels also use their musk to mark the borders of their hunting area, or territory. Should another weasel of the same sex wander inside these boundaries, the musk warns the intruder that it is trespassing and is not welcome. The scent is a secret message for other weasels. It tells them who lives there, how long ago they last visited this particular spot, and whether they are male or female. Female weasels also use musk to attract a mate.

When not raising a family, a weasel prefers to live alone.

Big Appetite

Imagine eating half your weight in food a day. That would mean that you would need 18 kilograms (40 pounds) of food a day if you weighed 36 kilograms (80 pounds). And that would be like eating 160 big hamburgers a day. Whew!

Although weasels are much smaller than we are, they *do* eat half their weight in food a day. As you can imagine, finding all that food is hard work.

Weasels do not eat vegetables. Only meat will do. The Least Weasel only eats mice, voles, insects and some amphibians. The ermine and Long-tailed Weasel also eat small rodents and insects, but squirrels, birds, eggs, reptiles, worms and rabbits add variety to their menu.

While hunting, the weasel relies even more on its keen sense of smell than on its eyesight.

Frozen Food

Just as squirrels gather nuts in the fall, weasels build up a large food supply for the winter. To do this, they take more prey than they can eat at one time. This helps to explain the weasel's reputation for being greedy.

The uneaten food is stored away in their burrow's special food storage room. To discourage any freeloaders from stealing, weasels scent this meat with their foul-smelling musk. This makes it very unappetizing to others.

Keeping stored food fresh is no problem. Because it is cold, the meat freezes. When weasels want to eat, they bring the frozen meat into their fur and grass-lined bedrooms. Soon, their body heat thaws the meat and they can eat. But however much food weasels store, they almost always run out. To find more, they hunt all winter long.

Tiny Terror

When it comes to hunting, you have to admire weasels. Few animals can match their skill and daring. They show little fear, and many will not hesitate to attack animals much bigger than they are.

Considering their small size, weasels are incredibly strong and agile. A weasel has no difficulty dragging a rabbit. To match this feat a lion would have to haul an elephant!

When chasing smaller game, weasels have a great advantage over larger predators. Their slender, tube-like bodies not only allow them to move with lightning speed, but they can also follow their prey right into its den, using their whiskers to help navigate through the narrow tunnels.

Tireless hunters, weasels spend most of their waking hours on the prowl, sometimes moving so silently that they can actually snatch a bird resting on its perch! No wonder they are considered to be among the best hunters in the world.

Weasel paw prints

Front

Back

Mating Season

To attract a mate, the female deposits her musk around her home territory. This musk may smell awful to us, but to a male weasel it is a very attractive scent.

The Long-tailed Weasel and ermine mate in the summer, but the female does not give birth until the following spring. Least Weasels often mate in January or February and give birth the same spring. Sometimes they will have another litter later in the summer.

Where snow cover is uncommon, the ermine may remain brown all year.

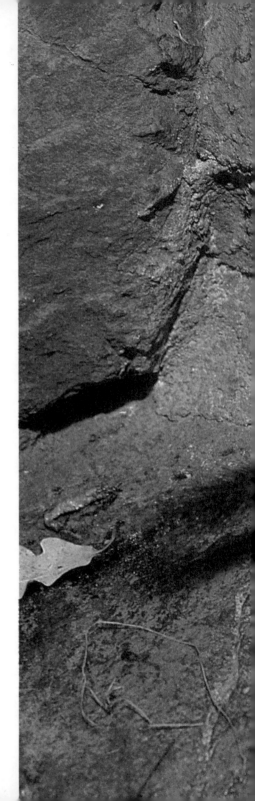

Meet the Babies

Before her babies are born, the female weasel prepares a nursery. Usually she digs out a special chamber in her den and makes a nest out of grass, feathers and fur. In this soft, warm nest three to 12 young are born.

What peculiar looking babies they are! Each one is pink and wrinkled. Their eyes and ears are sealed shut. They are entirely helpless and dependent on their mother.

At first the weasel babies live solely on their mother's milk. But before too long they are ready for solid food. The young weasels have an enormous appetite. They eat more than their body weight each day. Supplying all this food keeps their mother very busy.

Bright-eyed babies.

Play School

Once their eyes open at four to five weeks, the young weasels are very playful. They jump and tumble with each other, squeaking and squealing as they attack. Playing together is more than just fun. It helps to build the young weasels' muscles and teaches them valuable lessons about hunting. After all, pouncing on a brother or sister is not all that different from attacking a mouse.

But although the young weasels get stronger and more agile by the day, their mother is very protective of them. If any predator comes near, the mother weasel will courageously try to chase it off. She may even carry the babies away from danger one by one in her mouth.

The young grow very quickly. By age two to three months, they leave their mother and begin to hunt for themselves.

Catch Them If You Can

Tooth for tooth and gram for gram, the weasel is among the most ferocious animals in the world. What it lacks in size it more than makes up for in courage and boldness. Unbelievable as it may seem, a weasel no bigger than a kitten will attack a bear or a man standing in the way of its young.

Few animals care to tangle with such a determined foe. However, the weasel's own relatives—the mink, marten and fisher—are equally fierce and quick. These relatives will hunt weasels, as will foxes, bobcats, lynx, coyotes, wolves and larger hawks and owls.

Fortunately, the weasel has a great advantage over most of its enemies. It has an amazing ability to escape through the tiniest of openings. Have you ever heard the term "to weasel out of it"? This expression means to get out of something you do not want to do. It is easy to see how this saying began since nobody can "weasel" out of trouble like a weasel! Thanks to this amazing ability, weasels may live to be five to six years old in the wild.

Opposite page:

Weasels often sit on their haunches to get a better view of the world around them.

Friend Not Foe

Biologists tell us that if it were not for weasels, rats and mice would multiply so rapidly that they would overrun the world. As it is, mice cost us a tremendous amount each year in damaged crops. Weasels know what to do with these pests. One male alone can kill at least 500 mice a year! Their ability to catch small rodents would put any cat to shame. They are such good mousers, in fact, that their family name *Mustelidae* means "those who carry off mice."

Weasel Lore

North America's Native People have always had great respect for the weasel's fiery spirit. The Indians believed that the capturing of a weasel promised good fortune. In Inuit culture, some consider it good luck to have a weasel cross their path, and a young hunter sometimes carries a weasel pelt on his belt in the hope that he will inherit some of this animal's hunting skills.

Should a weasel ever race by you, try this trick. Stay perfectly still and make a squeaking sound by kissing the back of your hand. Chances are its curiosity will win out and it will reappear. You might just get a better look at one of nature's most graceful but secretive mammals.

Special Words

Amphibians A group of animals that lives both on land and in water. Frogs, toads, newts and salamanders are amphibians.

Biologist Scientist who studies animals and plants.

Burrow A hole in the ground dug by an animal to be used as a home.

Den Animal home.

Litter Group of animal brothers and sisters born together.

Marsh Soft wet land.

Mate To come together to produce young.

Mating season Time of year during which animals mate.

Musk A strong-smelling odor produced by some animals.

Predator Animal that lives by hunting others for food.

Reptiles A group of animals that includes such animals as snakes, lizards and turtles.

Territory Area that an animal or group of animals lives in and often defends from other animals of the same kind.

INDEX

Cover Photo: Wayne Lankinen (Valan Photos)

Photo Credits: Phil Dotson (National Audubon Society Collection/Miller Services), pages 4, 7, 12-13; Gregory Dimijian (National Audubon Society Collection/Miller Services), page 8; Barry Griffiths (Network Stock Photo File), page 11; Tom McHugh (National Audubon Society Collection/Miller Services), pages 14, 25, 35; Alvin E. Staffan (National Audubon Society Collection/Miller Services), page 17; Norman Lightfoot (Eco-Art Productions), page 18; Thomas Kitchin (Valan Photos), page 21; Wayne Lankinen (Valan Photos), pages 22, 45; Mildred McPhee (Valan Photos), page 27; Leonard Lee Rue III (National Audubon Society Collection/Miller Services), page 28; C.G. Hampson (Valan Photos), pages 32-33; Alan Carey (National Audubon Society Collection/Miller Services), pages 36, 41; G.R. Higbee (National Audubon Society Collection/Miller Services), page 42.